BANJO'S INSIDE COYOTE

-poems-

KELLI ALLEN

C&R Press
Conscious & Responsible

C&R Press
Conscious & Responsible
www.crpress.org

For special discounted bulk purchases, please contact:
C&R Press sales@crpress.org
To book events, readings, and author signings, please contact: info@crpress.org

BANJO'S INSIDE COYOTE

A Note of Thanks

Every tale begins with a nod to the five great directions. Sometimes, the head leans closer East than it does North and the eyes follow suit. In making the poems gathered in this book, I found my own glances circling wide and pausing often to memorize a sea, a fishing village in Connemara, the weathered hooves of an old plow horse in Granada, the sharp line of a lover's jaw, my own wrist caught by sand and fading daylight. Every detail marked in this collection is owed to the patience and support of my companions, both present and scattered amidst the swirl.

My Pirate reminds me daily of what Constantinos P. Cavafis wrote: "When you set sail for Ithaca, wish for the road to be long, full of adventures, full of knowledge," and for this I am especially grateful.

The scraggly yellow dog has not yet finished his jig and I remain, as ever, indebted to those who allow me time and space to watch the dance and add what I may to the Story.

It's hard to grasp how much generosity
Is involved in letting us go on breathing,
When we contribute nothing valuable but our grief.

Each of us deserves to be forgiven, if only for
Our persistence in keeping our small boat afloat
When so many have gone down in the storm.

—Robert Bly

Table of Contents

A part of three

A part of one

Now it was only the rivers
that spoke of the rivers,
and only the wind that spoke of its bees,
while the unpausing factual buds of the fruit trees
continued to move toward their fruit.

—Jane Hirshfield

Sailing with hermits means poverty, tribulation, and
discretion at every meal

Storms retire when the calmest sea lays down its head
on our desk made from oak and stag bone. The veins

hibernate salt heavy through dawn, through clumsy harbors
waving the last ships down. We think nets stay cast

in any weather and happy knees are those splinter carved
while the master sleeps. Every cell in the asylum has a bed

too soft for us. Admit right- and wrongdoing the way a basket
opens flat bottomed for butter caught against unfloured dough.

There are other lists than the ones you find in service; the names
that begin each page want to explain a magnificent unraveling.

Some chasms are too wide for any bridge runners to leap. From space,
crevices are spines disconnected, vertebra stretched out to grip and join

nothing. Where are your hands after morning prayers? The forest burns
itself so that white ash becomes a bowl for yeast and forgetting.

How To Tell You What Restraint Means

Mirabi says elephants know the way
down each mountain. Valleys pass
in supplication under such feet.

Between the clover and crabgrass, Vandeventer,
grackles arching in heat above, and one thick
wounded earthworm at your toe.

Reluctance is measurable: a glance toward you,
and two thousand blinking nods converge
to shout *Everyone runs away in the end!*

Let's agree to wedging eggshells into belly meat.
Whose fault is it when this pauper refuses a princess
lunch from his beaten violin case? Music, too, is blameless.

When the parrot reclines on his therapist's chaise
and weeps, the one asks the other: *are you certain*
you do not need the cracker? Desire only repels the alarm.

Sometimes the break is the seduction. Pennies
cover nipples at dawn leaving the eyes naked,
waiting for branches to lower, scrape, and claim.

Wild dogs howl love letters in Arkansas

Horses break every last thing about being in the dark
when their braying is less symphonic than a season
kindled in laying brick. Along this road are saddles
too wide for hips knowing lovemaking dawn until evening.

Riders circle the carnival and we slide the carpaccio between
us like men and women who know how to handle the reins.
If I die tonight, gather cherry pits from their flesh and make mounds
in these crystal bowls for the singers already on their way into town.

We plan the exact moment the comet crosses our periphery.
Your mouth over mine means miles well past the marked trail. Cross
the logs in this fire for wild old men who still lick their lips
when calves flash and wrists flail hard outward toward the barman.

Bitterness is the marrow left too long on the bone, never landing soft
in broth, parting tongue from speech, pleasure above hunger
while we sing two more poems, don't listen to the meter, and wedge
ankles under iron in the Southern heat of this moonless Sunday.

It does not matter whose name you call out when waking, or how quick
I receive "no." No other stone marks your chest sienna. The clumsiest facts
mean a quiet argument won in stitched tulips at your throat. Left hand or right,
palms circumvent the brow's need to suddenly, predictably lower.

Stilettos Can Wait By the Door

This will be a love letter after slipping
into, zipping fast, the tent. Calibrate how
gravity draws one feather over a bone.

Poles snap through rungs and you
do not notice my spine curl away.
The wrapped hatchet signifies want,
but not yours for me. Rather, where handle

meets steel reminds us both—we have been here
before. We agreed to keep your chairs behind doors
to which you have not once offered me a key. An albino
between teeth, dahlias do not mark grace.

I've shot over the wick and missed ignition the way
black and white photos line your daypack—dangerous
when the ballerina reaches in, slips *fouetté rond de jambes*
past us both. We can only teach each other a simple dance,

purpose the corset for what's good. We might burn
those maps after all. Maybe walking backward is boarding
a vessel meant to be outrun. What I know is your belt
undoes the high grasses I pretend are perennial and ours.
There is no palladium erected when you sleep.

Banjo's Inside Coyote

Scotch eggs, he says, complicate the sequence
between jaw bones and wet bellies. Two for me,
one for you, and the devil rows the boat on anyway.

We are field mice when alone. When the wrong horse
lowers, wives know to gather eggs for tomorrow's breakfast
early. The dog rolls bread between his paws and looks to the fire.

He barks, so we listen over rivers breaking dams, or tarns filling
fast with jarflies. *Giraffes have two hearts: one for the spleen's thick*
work, the other meant for birth waters puddling dirt under hooves.

All gods require renewal. There are coffins for goats, and urns
for barn owls begging the fool. There is no carnival fit to protest
a recipe shared from lighthouse to ships lined into armada.

Fur licked into plaits, catgut strings 'round those grinning teeth, our hound
sings over cold evening rituals. *Ladies, lovers, washbasin architects:*
Termites are the keepers of slow fires. Nothing wants to be the monster.

The price is the pearl you buried

It is not primitive to lick
lips when the foxes catch
a tail in their teeth. I have
stapled pages together so you,
too, might remember burrowing.

This is not about reconciliation. We mine
the softest ores first, but only
because the bones were not always
this hollow, tunnel-tight.

My Nafs refuse to run fast enough
to win any races. Perhaps they know
that drinking all night with a friend
is enough to feed the boat into its stream.

This morning I looked at your sleeping face
and instantly threw my maps
into the brush pile. We will spend
each night stealing mice from the silo.

Sweet water then, darling

Rowanberries painted against your wrist means
Open. Turning the ash-shrub blooms to face
your own chest reminds wet paper to unfold
from pocket to stone lain in evening sun. Midgard

knows two serpents. Between that world
and this one, it does not matter where
consumption begins. We tumble over ship's bow
looking too close for what tugs at the oxen head.

Neither cat nor whale lifts enough hide to defy
a well-cast net. *Let's reach the surface together*
you say. And I want to ask who will hold the bronzed
cup over my head as venom comes, torrential.

We are forgiven and burning. Blizzards are nothing
gradual after certain seasons work their stories, flawed
and shedding skins. One hand extends collected ash,
the other goes to work and tells no one how narrow this gate.

Honeycombs Light Cathedrals Upward Like Stars

We covet sweetness with or without
a guide. Smuggling tiny orange horses
across a body or border is still violence.
When did you stop collecting enough wax
to set aside, slick carpet honey light, for birds
left near-to-inconsolable? Beaks, sharp

hooked, do the damage before down dries
from one egg to the next. Murder again incubates
as patience. It remains easier to consume than bury
what might be dead soon enough. Too often
your kingdom grows smaller the closer your feet come
to a hearth. We have made ourselves both hammer

and softening birch. Still, pretend *alone* spells *waiting*
and never *failure.* A richer forest, then, hives nestled higher,
might be where you are headed. What breaks, gurgles open near
the station, is the very crust hardening around those lights, sticky
in your undeserving palms. Tell me now how to blame harmless direction.

An asterisk for the weather

I open wider when your hips circle close.
There is no storm, unstrapping its gales,
ruinous enough to hide your body from mine.
Not this night. Not morning, either, knitting
light into shoulder blades exposed, tendons
folding as hands supplicant, fingering
only bone meeting bone. The sea bean cord
slung around my throat signifies theft. A tongue
tip remembers salt in all five directions. So,

when you notice the sheets crippled
between cocked knees, consider how long
I wait to admit what a year means. Think
of how many times I offer you the nectarine
sliced even and sure, spread nautilus round
over beveled glass. Your appetite, my chest—
both rising as a fist meant to fit against
the fucked-up keyhole we mistake for wolves'
jaws. Depending on where you release, I might

say your name, and those birds we wept over
the first afternoon will swoop into the country
as though nothing here matters. But, darling—
there is only the width of this bed before
we spill through. I'll swallow what's left,
listening to the way we do anything for more,
thinking we have surrendered just this once.

There are three women in the back of the canoe, and each
one knows your name

When was the last time you traded your eyes
for a deer's, or a wolverine's just come
from the wood? If you look down
now, you might notice the red feathers
dropped wet from women's bellies, wombs
emptied and filling again, but not with your story
or seed. We make trouble everywhere
we go, ankles snapping under our boots.

How easy to forget leaning our back against
birch, ambition tucked under the bed, hunters
out early in morning, and our job to listen
well after the uncle severed bow from string.

Discipline has two partners, but we watch
only wildness in geese and ignore jaws
fang-lined and opened, half-mooned
in our periphery. So, when the hand slips
the brass, belt undone, borrowed eyes closing,
palm meat-full and beginning a rhythm

kept before any wedding song you have known,
tell me: which bride will notice your slicked
thigh and which will devour you whole,
river water whirling in behind her teeth?

If I could be a rib's width holding wrist to side

Another man might not notice
how many tawny frogmouths
occupy a nest. The inclination
to say as much unsticks
us both from an afternoon
sweet, entering lighter bones
than expected. In this city

crusted-over, an amputation
you predicted, I swim closer
anyway, to you, who never
takes my hand, instead pushes
one shoulder to furnish
a bridge between not quiet
and the watercolor I won't show
in any summer light. Murdering

only two impulses a day
means that your patience roots,
slow gallops past this chest
into a gut holding many rooms,
and you'll prove claims exactly
seven words. Not for open but for beneath,
and everything, scars ripped wire tight,
just as suddenly burns as falls, finally, asleep.

Damage doesn't know what debris spells
when the cedar floors occupy a chest
and not the house we don't live in
together. We believed in ghosts

in the village, and again in this city,
when the streets are a dream, too large
for closing distances. Walking through
landscapes means hearing frogs on concrete,
in rough puddles, and under the wood-
wrecked steps leading everywhere.

The birds are probably correct to assume
fallacy anyway. They repeat and sing
for what decomposes beneath such notes.
I handed my sword to the second watchman
while he hummed along, vocal trajectory
as snow slow collecting over hothouse orchids.

We imitate teachers regardless of temperature.
Did you know that the sun has been stolen
exactly twice? The story turned its back,
not away, but to the hard ground, and we left
tiny copper rings at each tree's thick base,
making promises to write new vows
for what slips into adoration. We are bodies
ever-flexing for meant declarations.

A part of two

So we all love a wild girl keeping a hold
On a dream she wants.

—Carl Sandburg

Ignore the priest's blessed drink, and we pull the bucket from the
sweet well too soon

This is how the screen manipulates:
I gather active and collect silence.

Of the five sips, this is the third. Tell me
When the feather slips cup into lips

Into gut. Explain this version of you—
Binary instead of voice, irrelevancies,

Regardless posture. See? We have married
Every drake bridging, wings extended hard,

These ponds. Still, feasts devoured
And mead tucked wet into belly, I know

How you look at me in afternoon light.
Consummation is communion only

After you admit, round eyes watching
My throat, that we are here. We are here.

The dilemma is how we crawl indirectly into sun

There is a point between middle finger's tip
and palm's sponged base where the length
of you fits. This holding is our penumbra,
a territory absent. Even Hephaestus, crazed,
her tenuous eyes upward and out, notices
what firms plump from stem to nail. At night

this does not matter. Only brackish afternoon,
when illicit means opening, when mares swallow
apples past their nine square teeth, and I salt
your thigh, disengage from pedagogy, excuse,
justification into the simple, pulled tight closer, want.

There is no ladder to lean against and we have counted
from Apollo to Tarsus in mimicry. We grip, for ill or good,
what's most likely to abandon us. This leaves only
an interstate backing our river. This leaves vinegar
rimming the pot, butt up to sugar, bent as a face seen first
through beveled glass, a bauble next, tongued fur to throat.

Svalinn: learning the names for shield

Eventually, ruin will stencil itself letter-by-
letter into upholstery already ripped, gaping
cotton bellies from the backseat of the car
you won't let me enter, lean against, starched
dress excluded. Later, I might tremble under

whichever palm you slide over my hip. Wreckage
is just another word for gardening. I had to make
up a tangible kingdom once hypnosis lifted, flattened
as taffeta smoothed over, blister free and marking
the other side of this spine, those failed woods.

We spill and collect, sometimes so close, rivering
into storm doors you painted shut. I expect a cliff-
ringed swirling with hammerheads below and ships
reflected above, where sky might have been through fog,
gray wolves cloud running instead, holy, fettered prayers.

Not Gary, Indiana

Some road trips are propelled by an arrow of indifference. We look
for the keys on their ring, nestled often in a bag of felid mice. If
my open sweater signifies *carry*, tail and tuft and brass also mean *rest*.

When we drove past the circus hand's kitchen, open in the way
of Southern Indiana late summers, we smelled peaches burning
on the rough iron stove. I remembered when you told me
that every day is a sliding between an expectation and an opening.
It was easy to hand over every coin in my purse and burn both
our tongues with pit fruits and cheap bourbon.

It doesn't matter that the wine you later spilled down my shoulder
blades was closer to blush than red—the ruin marked an embrace
I waited for all afternoon.

On the way to Fountain Square, I thought of astronauts, rushing
upward, cupping gloved hands over what might be heart or lungs
or just bones carapace-inward. You kept me steady with one hand
at my waist and I pretended to trust you, while we tiled chins toward
pinking sky, watching for satellites, certain, transformative.

It is illegal to take a Buddha out of the country. So, we are safe
when we remove only ourselves from these storefront nooks
and cross the steel tracks with our hands in each other's pockets.

Trishula could wend downward into the belly

Invention is strategy, and I say throw it into the pond
anyway. There is a room singing through a keyhole

welded bottom-to-top into knives. Blaming weeds
for lung fullness is a pastime. This is where rabbit runs

from hole to pretense to kindness to under tablecloths
set map-thin over banquets, welcoming what chokes.

We are mustangs in heather, hooves cutting thistle roots
to collect between vellum, history something else entirely.

There are instructions for monstrosity. Remember when light
was malleable and consoling meant fitting claw over tissue

to crosshatch what the branding iron missed? Admit you can sleep
now. Maybe we'll kiss the pins segregating, these, our blackbird spines.

Behind the boy on his knees
After Ocean Vuong

Attacking St. Paul means we deform the psyche backward.
Letting the Gnostics live gives permission to play songs
with spongy lips wrapping brass in a thick "O." Your mouth
pressed long into the center, dragging fingers close to meet
some rhythm determined before I agreed to this taking,
is a contract between the wren of my throat and the open lily

drowning other lovers in a tangle toward pond's bottom silt.
Even old church doors pile one atop the other to greet fire sending
orange smoke upward. Gods limp after collecting teeth all afternoon
in the dreams you won't mention past dark. What in you remains
despicable? The bare metal is rough to the breast, but this does not matter.

You are mounted anyway and do not need rope from my stern to moor
vessel or sail against such necessary wind. Even so, it is not four am
and what is left of your assumptions maps twin islands over my thighs. It's true
that we sweat through October. Remember, origami swans bend their tails
east.

The tortoise shell maps every star

No bull knows the thickness of its own rough horn. Some
blue jays steal only the scarecrow's left foot, and, like us,
he is left leaning too far against husks. There is a war

in the attic. Hounds' jaws lining baseboards,
silk windless in every corner, hemming
shut what we leave open each winter.

Disregard bundled egrets. We know better
than to trust feathers or beaks in tessellation.

The zodiac is a tablature you pocket for storms
at sea. When two calves are archboard painted,
the closest shore will never be to the east.

I have flown the absentee pennant, not noticing
moth appetites until both sun and setting moon
cooed pinpricked lights across unfurled backstays.

Barley and snakeroot in the same barrel means
jealousy, indicates reluctant shepherds will gather
both at dusk and in the softer curl of virgin morning.

Let's not go on pretending that disquietude is anything
chaste. There are miles urged open past this undertow
and we swim steady, siphoning wind, aerialists in the salt.

All I can see burning, and no reflection

Robberies are often quiet.
Our hands are in the air
while we sleep and the silo
empties twenty grains
at a time. When the chamber
echoes a hungry belly,
we pay attention only
to how deep our cups, how thin
our woven mats and cricket
high grass. I wonder

at nobility. There are four crowns
for taking, sacks open over
the well's lip. Remember
when everything after
the saddle meant asking
to be wanted? You, too, are Tiresias—
the staff you hold burns figs
as they leave branches to baptize
some sand too long in the sun.

Conversations from Luquillo to Boston, following the wrong dog home

Fair roof, dripping hall—these are names for *sky* where there should be only helmets left in the sand. We waste words mapping distance from one church to another, when religiosity is Fenrir in the north, and fresh birthed inkings, rooted in south sea brine. This is the way with us: Pythagorean stubbornness while we square the same four city blocks and discuss, too fast, our respective shames, walnuts quick meeting fire, and our first model ships.

You told me a story twice—once after collapsing against rough surf, and again while squinting into your first raw oyster. I learned both times that Vasilisa pulled up her hood and the rain came anyway and there is nothing too affected when staring hard, looking up through thick lashes. My answers to your questions were the same, too. Listening to Shuman propels all cattle directly into foam every time they get a craving for salt. Local fishermen near Luquillo assured us that hooves carry the beasts just fine over dune or mud. These men told us, in a round something like folksong, that the seaweed populating a wake is called *mane of the field*. At this, you collected a razor clam as it tunneled down and offered the pearlescent shell in an open palm.

This is the way Cézanne asks us to drown.

On the plane you close your eyes and change everything. I won't tell you how to skewer a raspberry to keep it whole, and you won't look at my mouth and remember that you might have fallen hard if we had stayed quiet longer.

It's alright that you do not wake when I remove the bone pin from your cloak. What sets us apart, like Archimedes, is the way we assert ourselves in each city: our occupation remains only to firm fit one set of fingers over another, anchors locked in oak and lapis, to signal, eventually, we are already *away*.

An origin story for satsuma mandarins in November

We swallow and never spit. Not once. Layers
go down and catch in threes. Seaweed carries

each fingerling bulb to bursting. Flesh pockets
inward first, reversing the fist. You have ridden

both waves: the brine thick in sand, and muscles
thigh-tight to wide break pelvis after pelvis.

Sticklebacks whittle pulp from stem to rind
and the bottom grouper just gapes his maw.

Sturgeon trouble crawlers back from wet land
so every reach is a collecting, a gathering close

what the King named *ball fit for the stew.* Wait
for Taurus to cough the arrow feather into a stream.

Eventually, we wrap both hands around something
beloved. Even worse, *seedless* means nothing to re-read.

Inward crows order baubles for the nest

On your back, well-lived and disappearing,
stomach a skyline curtain swaying in some

new cold. Later, we will die in the same way—
awake or not, gathering from the body first.

Jesuits insist we own nothing save voice
and original fur. Packages are cloudy or transparent.

When you woke, there was snow over fresh mud
signifying what we know to be escape waiting.

Someone else disturbs the hornblade mounted flush
to exposed brick. You will gesture surprise, a tentative

renouncing, whore-wide glance to window to ceiling
to clock pestered open when the world's spine is a bible, too.

When there are ostriches under amendments

When was the last time you rebuked
the one in you who wants something?
Go on asking. Even hermits listen
to the sitar player stringing the neck
tight after taverns in this city go dark.

The shadow has long hated the word "bliss"
and the old Zen masters refuse to dream
near sunset. This subconscious tells jokes
to the weaker giants who cannot yet climb
a witch's growth mountain. Samson's son dies

and blame combs back from our foreheads
long enough. Misfortune isn't theft or forgetfulness.
Salesmen come because our doors swing wide
outward, through six storms or twenty. It's only
too late for street corner Mary, for sophisticated sick.

Resolutions are horses corralled too long

How many stories
does a culture audition
before coal weds the wall?

Salmon eggs last only
four days in warming water.
Bears have sovereignty in times
when ancestors are sent quietly
into exile. This is courtship

under and above lily pads, greater
than any condition. In the presence
of a maiden's rice smile, no lizard
leaps directly into blue flames. Grief

between an aging king and his queen
means covetousness quakes and screams
slacked-jawed from nest to burrow.
Dusk-time is never the same for ravens

and hares. Gentleness will not come.
Eventually, anything loved is going to drown.

A part of three

If you don't become the ocean, you'll be seasick every day.

—Leonard Cohen

Following the wrong duck to deeper water

We are one counteragent to entropy; we are creatures
ramshackle, propulsion after severance, stillness before.

Rice falls into piles without an attendant, dispersed after palm-held
sand says no to the mandala, supplicant under wind. There are threads

apart with never a censure from women gathering close to the hearth.
The messenger loses his way in tall grass and this is about building a castle

that welcomes us past the gate. There will always be photos that fall
directly onto the path you most wish to map. Faces will not be your own

and this means seven bricks higher, layer over layer, for a parapet
no embroidery silver will capture. Entrances are the needles under

a reef when the mallards begin to circle, their eyes trained for water
you swam only once. We marry who steeps the wrong tea too long.

Demonstrations on leaving winter. Or, staying buoyant in this storm

Split the pelican's belly in half: one side for a purse,
the other to feed a yearling. I might be inadequately
hungry, but there, in the world, appetite billows first

and Heidegger slinks toward sandbars disappearing
East. Let's assure one another that errors are minnows
caught in the throat's thin net. Our childhood buttons

fracture after the first rough bite. There is not enough
bile in any stomach to wrench mother-of-pearl and hounds-
tooth to snow, to peat moss for the barrel. Embowed draws

bill-to-chest and what choice do we have but to consider
chastity in the mandible-tipped bag? I may beg you revive
every one of us curled in dirt at your feet. Will three days

distinguish hunger from sleep? You are set to carry that pack
far from what I want. Omission lowers your gaze past ankle,
toward wood floor grains and wool, just right, and I know

better than to ask after the red-haired lover whose council
keeps you flipping one screen dark and then another until both
brow and wrist succinctly map which way goes your wooden ship.

A tooth fingered into your white pocket

A lead starling instructs the first seven,
then another, larger group, and the spiral
begins in earnest. Mud baths keep shoulders

from forgetting the ground. This is longing,
too, and we don't need permission to tell stories.
When was the last time your mother died? Merchants

leave and the tutor learns to tie bonnets under
our chins, bowing the throat just so. In the afternoon,
we cry out because undertow between our thighs means

no more pillows to hide a key; wrists bitten to raw, singing.
Blueprints in sunflowers, or rooms behind fences: the Kitsune
bites his tail for every year we lose count of the rice, let broth

turn vinegar under eggshells we piled too high. A father's ship
sails when bamboo meets nailbeds. We are tender pink, marked
for North, and what spills into me washes your fingers in the morning.

Tortoises are unattached from snow in any city

Think about the second time you were crippled. Myths
cause trouble and stimulate our need for sleeping

all winter. The truth is that what wounds in some forest
slices through maps pocketed, too. Even if the angler

reminds us to keep lights on toward the sea, rounding
hands to binocular eyes, does not make a plenum smaller.

The crescendo is loneness sinking beneath a new address,
letters steepling high, reverence overtaking wrinkled stamps.

There is an anagram for your teeth against my pale belly. Just
as extending one neck out to collect berries for months ahead,

we do not once forget how lashes cling flat over damp January
cheeks. Burrowing through this weeping is how we chew *amen*.

Your head in my lap, afternoon discussing shells long overdue,
and the road just opens white, cold, going on faster, going at all.

You don't know your life anyway

It was early and the extension of you was less,
and wet, twitch thumping between my cheek
and your thigh. We'll go alone hunting spring elk.

We share certain heroes in the wild way epics
are memorized in classroom caves far south
of here. Curtains above my bed are a misunderstanding.

Pelicans reach far back into the throat, too. Knocking
light against oak means more than knuckles finding
copper pots, steel blades hinting at rust, at long nights.

How to answer questions on post-coital rituals at sea

On Jupiter, there are six nights for drinking rye. This leaves
only nine hours for beating, unfolding, and mouthing

what we think we know about oceans elsewhere. Burdens
for the sake of having means we stay half-woken, digestible

tremors symmetrical, a treaty made before Eurydice ensured
our favorite blindness. What is left inside my pockets seeds

nothing further than corset stains memorializing what comes
before mimosas, after rubbing telescope rings from both sets

of eyes. I have sold my way of speaking for shallows, sandbars
dotted and egg-thick. Every shell underneath is a hook and fuse

marking return, saying so few make it to the first tide intact.
These bodies, nets cast to collect wreckage, to mimic Esmeralda's gold.

Every Day Is A War Camp Under Cassiopeia

> My head floats
> in a washbasin.
> Let it be carried
> to the king.
> —Bill Meissner

The open mouth is a mead hall. You sob
toward the woods and no one who has eaten
elk liver comes between the birches to save you.

We are broken open by weather panels collected
in bone hollows—marrow long devoted
to arms thrown around too many kings.

There are four years wasted on marrying water
fowl, and two situated over someone else's rope
bridge. Pipe smoke for gorge moss means resignation,

maybe shame. Rotgut holds bile viper-coiled in throats
too long, and the upward gifts never make a path
clear for celebration. Exhale once with intention

and every hammock fills with sleepers facing Andalusia.
It does not matter with which hand we toss our only spear—
sometimes a scorpion tail numbs both wrists, beheading

our desire, carrying the silver pike far upriver. Every morning
we die twice. Pelicans hoard tiny needles for stitching sails
while we watch Hector wave over dust whirling up through sand.

Tell each other how to pick the locks from a mother's room
to her only son's burnt cradle. The words you promise complicate
a jackal's tongue into thick knots, letting what we deserve

harden into keyring and key. There is not a waist narrow enough
to belt this much absence. The months are thrown back down
and we sing anyway, beating coats over rocks, water swirled dark.

Avoiding the mirror beneath an oak means you disappear, too

The daughter fell into the raft of mallards,
an impatient tortoise rising from beneath.

Theirs was an island where we die for hours
stretched over the sun's mean wrinkles, thick face

peeking from our nailbeds and callouses.
There are four women for each sycamore. Acorns

fill stomachs empty all summer, and we read indexes
looking for grandiosity spelled-out in soft notes.

Someone may bring a badger to your bay window,
perhaps wiser than all your sisters, and those paws

will hold huckleberries and goblin shark teeth
collected while you slept through another storm.

When anyone comes to our door, forgives us,
we instantly let the child we carry on our backs

down onto the dirt floor to make circles with carrots
we whittled while surviving so many nights.

If I flinched at every grief, I would be an intelligent idiot

Wisdom sedimentary in a white hare's belly and your palm almond pressed
to the V that lights hearth from forest shades too close—symbols only insouciant

for the body blind, beggars turning alms to names spoken backward and once.
Singers' caves in Granada host the fox and bull, both, and what is meant

for feasting becomes smoke oiling ceiling to stack to wide, reflective skies.
Thrum eulogies and untie these robes: what this skin wants ritualizes morning,

sacred seeds wetting some new garden. We reject wine at the king's table
at such a cost. I am weak and the years are thick strings. Somedays, even

the cups are driven mad. Clutch whittled flutes to both chests and refuse to turn
around. What waits at one mouth waits at many. Who is listening, safe or certain?

The kisses I offer you are holy. They are the fire of the old gods. And as with all magic
things, this heat requires praise. Hold open your chest and tilt your cheek toward my lips.

We worship only once in this life.

Leather wraps both our shoulders, and I will call you my lungs,
my falconer, guidepost

We have swallowed the whole field. Tell me how to discover shovels
leaning less still, their names for metals happening later, closer to dusk.

I would give you buildings on fire, barn house doors ashed to moss, if you threw
one hand into the pond, pulled windowpanes back to shore. I know every moment

you tighten the other palm around horses kept miniature in my pockets. Our bodies
often possessed by place, fit one into the other under stained glass, borrowed warm.

Kingdoms don't need context to nestle further against hillocks. I have been writing
our story to measure how underwater, my mouth holds your throat softer, legs

untangling in the last chapter, waking our firebird too late. That past is image over
image is no accident. Your jaw aches through each night and October rains anyway.

The doe is a widow. We see her cross one hoof too rough into woodpecker nests
fallen before anything autumnal pronounced an hour for grief, or for sleeping.

Eventually, we accept stars' light as distance side-by-side. Abundance is forgiving,
is the carpet under my knees, and your chin dawn-lit, eyes closed against everything.

Galloping toward the harbor, crown in our pocket

When roots are horses, nothing seeds to fruition.
It is this way with us, too. We pass tasting booths
in Madrid and on the way down, pocket notes
meant for after curtains blunt wide. We leave applesauce
under the bedroom window in exchange for crow
feathers small enough to pick teeth white on purpose.

A landscape boxed is still one doe curled into her buck
and no chorus or apology proves this wrong. Smuggle
the dead into the theatre, wait for the third ovation—
the full moon does not always mean *wolf.*

Maybe you've seen them—the two knots left
on the wrist. Once, we were convinced venom
could be drawn from muscle to tongue to ground. Maybe
you remember the surface red, weeping, your hand
a paw too large against the satin. This is not a story
about impotent death. We have habits and photographs,

sometimes scars, for such embarrassment. I might hum
the notes of how we arrived, in which old boat, backs stiff,
becoming pine, too. Every sail is an eager geometry near wind.
In this murmuration, starlings build parapets from rising jungle
mist and somewhere in the noise, an invitation will fall
into your lap. You will gesture, break every conversation,
tiny bones pillaring beneath first one elbow and then the next

until the throne is cast for you to fall back and fall soft. Look
at the just-closing mouth, the proof slated for a ledger dug-up
and dusted with beetle carcasses meant for next week's rain.
What will we do with such a king and how will we welcome
you, robes so fresh, a pulse through the moss, into this body?

When the brother of the man I love says,
I wish I could spell cunt with a K

every window in this house rolls down as shades
suddenly liquid glass and each snort and breath
is a relief, an exhale into a day rough with ugliness,
all expectation against sleep and assumptions.

Something we touch, this absence, her hair,
and too soon here is the brother I collect
for telling—ridicule and hound fang ferocity
marking our new affection, the afternoon long

forgotten. We have wedged shoulders tight,
pretended to talk about nothing like cars rolling
a cage into waiting dirt, or fathers chasing woodchucks
under trailers lit with whisky. So when he steeples

both elbows on my table, eyes too wide, set apart
as on a buck's down face, caught close to some pond's slick
edge, and offers vulgarity as a plea, a thin wish to be carved
higher on the tribe's birch pole than the man I love, this not brother

of mine is passed the crown. I will not weld this found family
into a new crest for a mantle fire to lick and suckle. Instead,
I will curtsy and light three candles. We, too, are gratitude asunder
and games for night mean spit in the palms, pressed to morning.

Saying *morning* out loud, maple leaves fall anyway

Hair pinned back, broken barn a distant point
that serves as compass, as salve, and we are, again,
too easily alone. Which of us remember tender ruin,

sometimes the mother's locket, or the barley deep
in dry palms? The breeze fits a wolfman who never wanted
his moon, and you say *don't be sad* and I am havoc, weak

and careful. We hold the other only so long before glass
reclaims our backyard ship. The folksinger hears forecasts,
lyre nestled into his ribs, tight against November uncertainties.

For us, the seatop knows our timbre and we speak soft, often
enough to fool Coyote into thinking this story was his from
the start. We rescue each other when the orchard cools to sleep.

If you sleep, no one will die

Don't worry about it. Make a smaller boat, not
a larger one. How far does the bottom
arch, bowed long and tight, need to reach
before both your hands cup the vessel's
side and we take to the current together?

Bees hide only two things in the honeycomb:
The first queen's desire to flee, amber packed
and buried, and the flames started, but blown
almost out when your breath came too close.

I am lonely, too, but only because you chased
me from swift sand into Monet's bleak hut. Tell me
you might not leave in the morning
and neither of us will complain one time
about your father or mine or temporary descent.

What have you packed into that case shaped
like your neck at night, creased over silk, inadequately
furred? Show me what happens when pockets turn belly
out and we defy everything that does not make us jump
up and gobble the wounded, refuse again to lie down.

Acknowledgments

"The tortoise shell maps every star" and "All I can see burning, and no reflection" appeared in *The American Journal of Poetry*

"Lyrebird Keeps The Peace Between Moon and the Lover" appeared in *Sun Star Review*

"The price is the pearl you buried," "Sweet water then, darling," and "If you sleep, no one will die" appeared in *Sequestrum*

"There are three women in the back of the canoe, and each one knows your name" appeared in *New Territory*

"Conversations from Luquillo to Boston, following the wrong dog home" and "Not Gary, Indiana" appeared in *The Common*

"Ignores the priest's blessed drink and we pull the bucket from the sweet well too soon" appeared in *Abridged*

"Honeycombs Light Cathedrals Upward Like Stars" appeared in *MockingHeart Review*

"The dilemma is how we crawl," "Tortoises are unattached by snow," and "How to answer questions" appeared in *Poetry City*

"Stilettos can wait by the door" appeared in *Your Impossible Voice*

"*You don't know your life anyway*" appeared in *Pulp Literature*

"When the brother of the man I love says, *I wish I could spell* cunt *with a K*" appeared in *Red Fez*

"*If I flinched at every grief, I would be an intelligent idiot*," "If I could be a rib's width holding wrist to side," "Saying *morning* out loud, maple leaves fall anyway," "All I can see burning, and no reflection," and "When there are ostriches under amendments" appeared in *Blue Mountain Review*

C&R PRESS CHAPBOOKS

C&R Press hosts two chapbook selection periods from June to September and November to March coupled with a reading in New York City each year. The Winter Soup Bowl and Summer Tide Pool Chapbook Series are open to new and established writers in poetry, fiction, essay and other creative writing.

2018 Winter Soup Bowl
Paleotemptestology by Bertha Crombet
White Boys from Hell by Jeffrey Skinner

2017 Summer Tide Pool
Atypical Cells of Undetermined Significance by Brenna Womer

2017 Winter Soup Bowl
Heredity and Other Inventions by Sharona Muir
On Inaccuracy by Joe Manning

2016 Summer Tide Pool
Cuntstruck by Kate Northrop
Relief Map by Erin M. Bertram
Love Undefined by Jonathan Katz

2016 Winter Soup Bowl
Notes from the Negro Side of the Moon by Earl Braggs
A Hunger Called Music: A Verse History in Black Music
by Meredith Nnoka

C&R PRESS TITLES

NONFICTION

Women in the Literary Landscape by Doris Weatherford, et al
Credo: An Anthology of Manifestos & Sourcebook for Creative Writing by Rita
Banerjee and Diana Norma Szokolyai

FICTION

Made by Mary by Laura Catherine Brown
Ivy vs. Dogg by Brian Leung
While You Were Gone by Sybil Baker
Cloud Diary by Steve Mitchell
Spectrum by Martin Ott
That Man in Our Lives by Xu Xi

SHORT FICTION

Notes From the Mother Tongue by An Tran
The Protester Has Been Released by Janet Sarbanes

ESSAY AND CREATIVE NONFICTION

Immigration Essays by Sybil Baker
Je suis l'autre: Essays and Interrogations by Kristina Marie Darling
Death of Art by Chris Campanioni

POETRY

My Stunt Double by Travis Denton
Lessons in Camoflauge by Martin Ott
Dark Horse by Kristina Marie Darling
All My Heroes are Broke by Ariel Francisco
Holdfast by Christian Anton Gerard
Ex Domestica by E.G. Cunningham
Like Lesser Gods by Bruce McEver
Notes from the Negro Side of the Moon by Earl Braggs
Imagine Not Drowning by Kelli Allen
Notes to the Beloved by Michelle Bitting
Free Boat: Collected Lies and Love Poems by John Reed
Les Fauves by Barbara Crooker
Tall as You are Tall Between Them by Annie Christain
The Couple Who Fell to Earth by Michelle Bitting
Notes to the Beloved by Michelle Bitting

www.ingramcontent.com/pod-product-compliance
Lightning Source LLC
Chambersburg PA
CBHW031150090426
42738CB00008B/1282